For Ava With Love

This is the story of
Ava the Angel and how
she becomes a little baby girl.

One day in Heaven, God looks
upon all of his Angels.

He sees the adult Angels,
the pet Angels, the Grandma and
Grandpa Angels, and he notices
the baby Angels.

The baby Angels are playing in a field
of beautiful purple lilies.

He spots one of the baby Angels
who is bright, cheerful and
full of energy.

She plays well with the other Angels,
and she laughs a lot.

The Angel's name is Ava.

Ava's laugh is very contagious.
God chuckles as he watches
her play.

He asks his main Counselor
who sits on the right side
of his throne,
"Who is this baby Angel
who laughs much with her friends?"

His Counselor answers and says,
"Her name is Ava, which means,
'breath of life.' "

God has an idea. He knows
that Ava the Angel can bring
a lot of joy and happiness to the
people of the Earth through
her laughter and her love.

So, he decides to find the perfect
family to send Ava the Angel
to live with on Earth.

He searches high and
he searches low.
He looks in Africa and he looks
in Asia. He looks in Europe and
he looks in Australia.

He looks in South America,
North America,
the Caribbean and Hawaii.

One day, while God is searching,
he hears a prayer.
It is the prayer of a woman
that he knows very well.

God always hears her prayers.
So, he listens closely.

"Dear God," she says,
*"It's me again.
I really need your help.
I want to have
a child: a child that is healthy,
happy and can bring joy
to the lives of me
and my husband. Amen."*

When God hears
the woman's prayer,
he knows that she and her husband
are the perfect family for
Ava the Angel.

He is sure that Ava
will bring joy to their lives.
She will make them laugh and
she will bring happiness
into their home.

After God finds the perfect family
for Ava, he calls her out
of the field of lilies and asks,
"Ava, would you do me a big favor?"

Ava the Angel answers,
*"Yes God, I would do anything that
you ask. What is the favor?"*

God says, *"I need you to leave home
and go to the Earth to live with
a beautiful family that is in need
of an Angel like you."*

Ava the Angel looks at God
with a smile and says,
"Okay God, send me, I will go!"

Late one night,
while the woman sleeps,
God sends Ava the Angel
to her in the form of a tiny baby
inside of her belly.

Ava the Angel
grows for nine months.

One beautiful day,
Ava the Angel is finally born.

Her Mother holds her in her arms
while her Father looks upon
her beautiful face.

Her parents name her Ava Lillian,
which means the breath of life;
and beautiful lily of the field.

This is how Ava the Angel
becomes Ava Lillian.

And, God looks upon
the new family that he has
created and he is pleased.

Ava the Angel

Story by Allyson Ward Neal
Art by RMFlorendo
Design by Kim-Chi Le

Made in the USA
Monee, IL
05 November 2026

67377489R00017